better together*

* This book is best read together, grownup and kid.

a
kids
book
about

a kids book about

by Cousin Danny

A Kids Book About
Editor Emma Wolf
Head of Design Rick DeLucco
Publisher Jelani Memory

DK
Senior Production Editor Jennifer Murray
Senior Production Controller Louise Minihane
Managing Editor Hazel Eriksson
Publishing Director Mark Searle

This American Edition, 2026
Published in the United States by DK Publishing,
a Division of Penguin Random House LLC
1745 Broadway, 20th Floor, New York, NY 10019

Text and design copyright © 2026 by A Kids Book About, Inc.
'A Kids Book About' is a trademark of Dorling Kindersley Ltd.
'Kids Are Ready' and the colophon 'a' are trademarks of A Kids Co.
26 27 28 29 10 9 8 7 6 5 4 3 2 1
001—356887—May/26

All rights reserved. Without limiting the rights under the copyright reserved above, no part of this publication may be reproduced, stored in or introduced into a retrieval system, or transmitted, in any form, or by any means (electronic, mechanical, photocopying, recording, or otherwise), without the prior written permission of the copyright owner.

No part of this publication may be used or reproduced in any manner for the purpose of training artificial intelligence technologies or systems. In accordance with Article 4(3) of the DSM Directive 2019/790, DK expressly reserves this work from the text and data mining exception.

First published in Great Britain in 2026 by
Dorling Kindersley Limited, 20 Vauxhall Bridge Road, London SW1V 2SA
A Penguin Random House Company

The authorised representative in the EEA is
Dorling Kindersley Verlag GmbH. Arnulfstr. 124, 80636 Munich, Germany

A CIP catalogue record for this book is available from the British Library

ISBN 978-0-2417-9491-3

DK books are available at special discounts when purchased in bulk for sales promotions, premiums, fund-raising, or educational use. For details, contact: DK Publishing Special Markets, 1745 Broadway, 20th Floor, New York, NY 10019, or SpecialSales@dk.com

Printed and bound in China

www.dk.com

akidsco.com

This book was made with Forest Stewardship Council™ certified paper – one small step in DK's commitment to a sustainable future.
Learn more at www.dk.com/uk/information/sustainability

This book is dedicated to my sweet,
handsome nephew River James.
I'll always be here for you.

Intro
for grownups

Today's kids are moving less and feeling more overwhelmed than ever. The COVID-19 pandemic only deepened this struggle—disrupting routines, limiting social interaction, and drastically reducing physical activity. Many families saw firsthand the rise in anxiety, mood swings, and emotional stress.

Movement is one of the most powerful, yet overlooked, tools for supporting a kid's mental well-being. It helps reduce stress, improve mood, and build emotional intelligence. Whether it's dancing in the living room, climbing at the park, or just running freely, movement gives kids a healthy way to express emotions, release energy, and reconnect with joy.

This book offers simple ways to bring more movement into daily life, because when kids move, they don't just build stronger bodies. They build stronger minds, healthier hearts, and happier lives.

Hi! My name is
Danny Vuong-Batimana,
but most folks call me

COUSIN DANNY.

Movement is MY JOB,

MY PASSION,

and MY LIFE.

I THINK MOVEMENT IS THE

MOST IMPOR

TANT

THING IN THE WORLD.

But before I tell you why,
let me tell you a little about me...

I grew up in the ’80s, and I loved recess, hanging out with friends, and playing sports...

especially basketball!

I remember when the Los Angeles Lakers drafted Magic Johnson and I got to see him play.

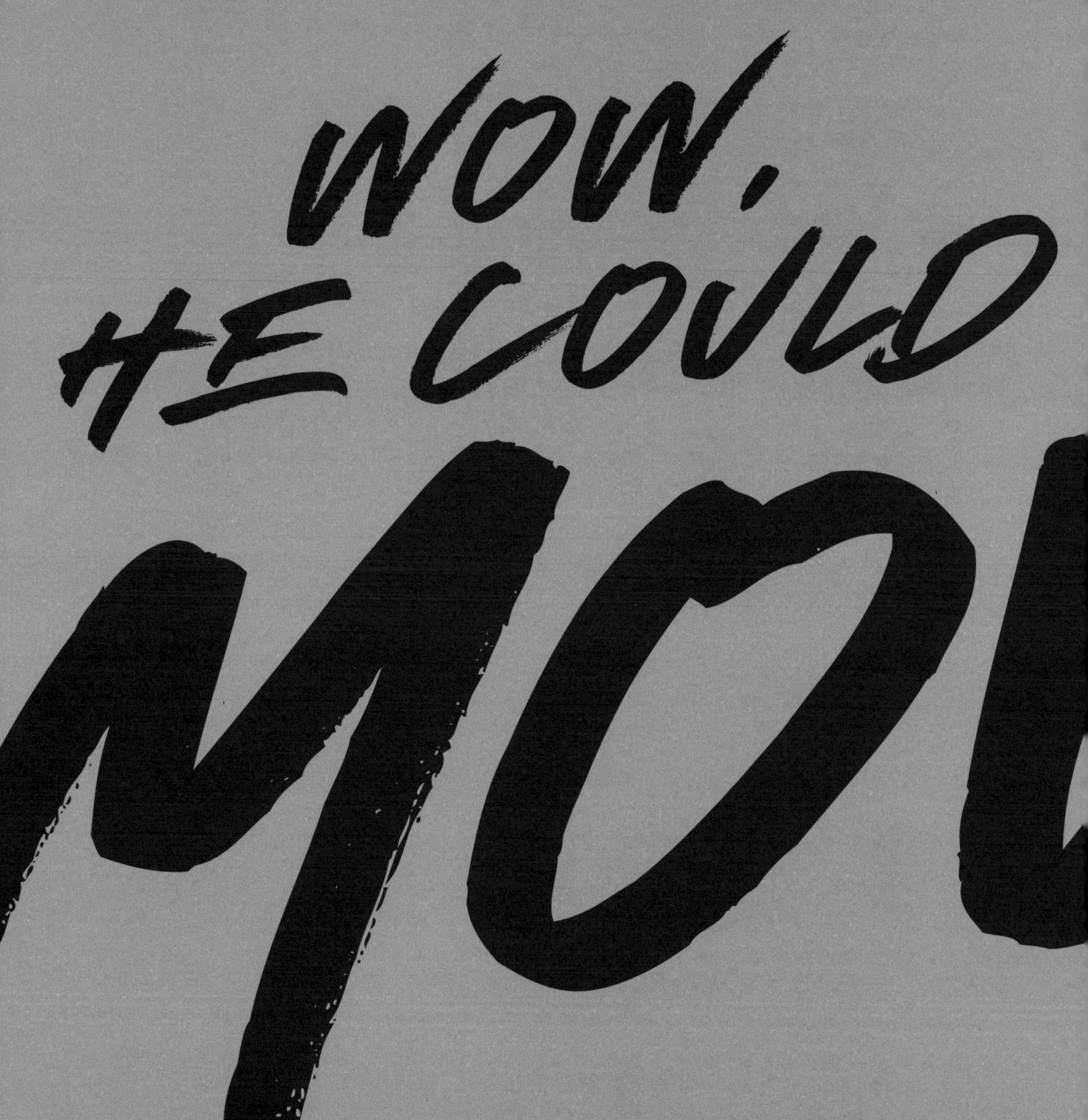

I became a lifelong Lakers fan
and fell in love with **movement**.

As a kid,
I loved moving in EVERY WAY.

I loved playing.

I loved basketball.

And, more than anything...

I LOVED TO DANCE!

I’m Filipino-American,
and proud of it.

There’s a saying that you
know you’re Filipino if you’re
a singer, dancer, or a nurse.

WELL, I WAS A DANCER!

I LOVED TO DANCE
SO MUCH!
AND I STILL DO!

I never missed a day of school
so I could teach my friends
the latest dances at recess.

When I was in high school,
I got to join the **dance team**.

I was never more happy than when I was **moving my body** and **dancing with my teammates**.

But... I always worried that the other kids wouldn't think

I was **insecure** because
I was the only boy on a
dance team full of girls.

And I was **afraid**, because
I was gay and wasn't ready
for anyone to know.

I didn't want to be judged or
not liked because of who I am.

But I pushed through, because

I LOVED DANCE SO MUCH.

And I'm glad I did,
because it was a blast.

Being on the dance team was how I got to show everyone what I could do.

I danced a lot, and I got pretty good.

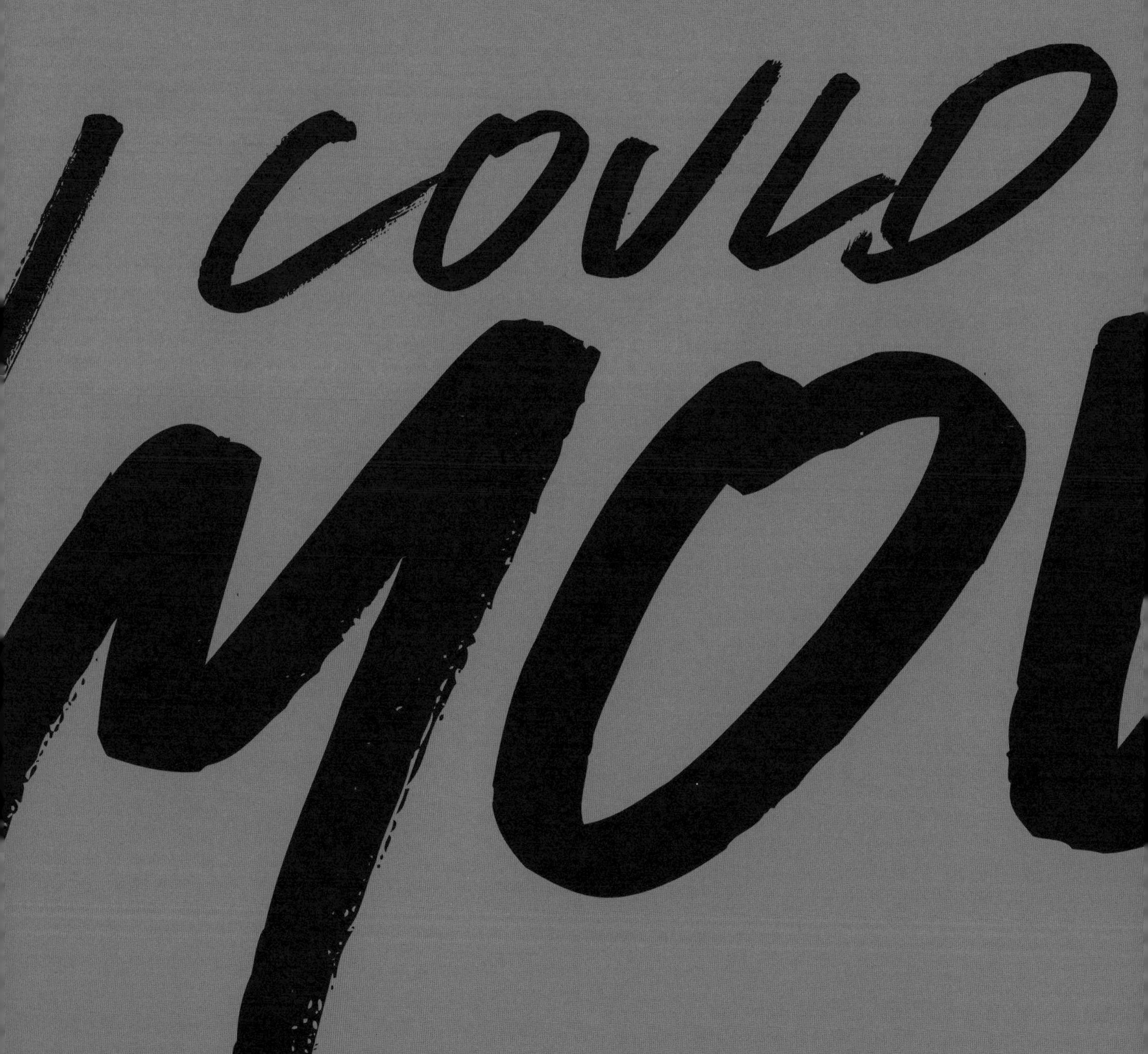

I could also **choreograph**, which is a fancy way of saying I could create dances for other people to do.

And one day, I got a
once-in-a-lifetime
opportunity.

Two of my friends were now dancing for the **Lakers**.

Yes, the same **LA Lakers** I had loved since I was a kid!

They had just gotten two of the
best players in the world,
Shaq and **Kobe**!

I got to **design** and **choreograph** some of the dances the Laker Girls did.

I even got to choreograph for the Portland Trail Blazers and the Los Angeles Clippers.

Basketball and dance together?

YES, PLEASE!

I got to live my dream of dancing for an audience and teaching others to dance, too.

Eventually, I even found the courage to come out as my full self.

A LOT

TO

MENT.

To me...

MOVEMENT IS THE NUMBER ONE THING IN LIFE.

And guess what?
There are *SO* many ways to move!

Walking, running, swimming, dancing, playing soccer—it doesn't matter how you move, because it's all

SOME:

But, not every every kind of movement is for everyone.

So, here's some advice I give my nephew River James!

Tennis, rock climbing,
or gymnastics.

Lifting weights, walking
a dog, or riding a bike.

And if you don't like it...

It's OK to say,
"That's not for me."*

*River James also likes to wave his index finger "no" when he says this—you can try that too!

But if you do like it,
keep going!

And don't be afraid to
try something weird,
or new, or different.

Try moving to music.

Put on your favorite song and just feel.

HOW DOES YOUR BODY WANT TO MOVE?

Actually, go ahead and put down this book and go try that right now!

I'LL WAIT

FOR YOU!

Once you discover a bunch of ways you like to move, make a list!

Seriously, grab a piece of paper and start writing it down!

See how long that list can be.

THEN, SHARE YOUR FAVORITE MOVES WITH SOMEONE.

Show them what you can do,
and see if they can do it too!

Everyone has different **abilities**, **skills**, and ways movement feels right for them.

Not everyone can move in the
same way, and that's **OK**.

But however you move...

why

Because movement
is key to living a **long**,
healthy, and **purposeful life**!

I’ve spent my whole life moving,
and here’s what I’ve learned:

MOVEMENT MAKES YOU

HAPPY.

MOVEMENT MAKES YOU

STRONGER.

MOVEMENT MAKES YOU

KINDER.

Movement is a way to **communicate**, **connect with others**, and **connect with yourself**.

And here’s the thing:

IF YOU DON'T USE IT, YOU LOSE IT.

So, use your body and ***MOVE!***

Any chance you get, *MOVE!*

Even if it's a little, or a lot.

It doesn't matter...

Outro
for grownups

You were made to move! Whether you're dancing, running, playing, or just wiggling your fingers, every move helps your body and brain feel better. Movement gives you energy, helps you focus, and lifts your mood when you're feeling down.

In the busyness of life, it's easy to feel more tired, stressed, or stuck. But guess what? Moving again—just a little each day—can help you feel strong, happy, and confident. If you don't use it, you lose it, so keep your body and brain working by using them in fun, active ways!

Your challenge: Pick one way to move today. Dance to your favorite song, go swimming, walk your dog, or play your favorite game outside.

Then do it again tomorrow. And the next day.

You got this!

About The Author

Cousin Danny (he/him) wrote this book for his nephews, River James and Nio, and his goddaughter, Ava.

As a kid, Cousin Danny discovered that movement helped him feel focused, joyful, and confident. He'd wake up early just to get to school in time to move, dance, and play—it became his superpower!

Today, Cousin Danny shares that same passion through Cousin Danny LIVE!, a dance-based assembly program that inspires thousands of kids each year. After the pandemic, his mission grew even clearer: movement supports wellness, learning, kindness, and inner strength.

He believes everyone has the power to move—and if you don't use it, you lose it.

Let's move!

@cousindannylive

Cousin Danny LIVE!

www.cousindannylive.com

Made to empower.

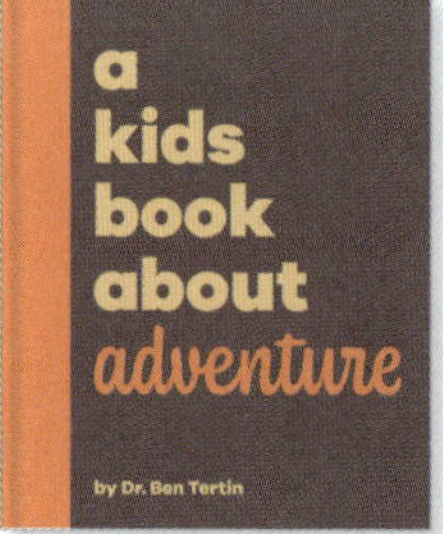

Discover more at akidsco.com